BIG SPORTS BRANDS

SPORTS ILLUSTRATED

Leader in Sports Media

by Gail Radley

SportsZone

An Imprint of Abdo Publishing
abdobooks.com

abdobooks.com

Published by Abdo Publishing, a division of ABDO, PO Box 398166, Minneapolis, Minnesota 55439. Copyright © 2024 by Abdo Consulting Group, Inc. International copyrights reserved in all countries. No part of this book may be reproduced in any form without written permission from the publisher. SportsZone™ is a trademark and logo of Abdo Publishing.

Printed in the United States of America, North Mankato, Minnesota.
052023
092023

THIS BOOK CONTAINS RECYCLED MATERIALS

Cover Photo: Stanley Weston/The Stanley Weston Archive/Archive Photos/Getty Images
Interior Photos: John Biever/Sports Illustrated/Getty Images, 4–5; MediaNews Group/The Mercury News/Getty Images, 6; Tom DiPace/AP Images, 7; Carolyn Kaster/AP Images, 9; Rusty Kennedy/AP Images, 11; Picture Post/Hulton Archive/Getty Images, 12–13; Santi Visalli/Archive Photos/Getty Images, 14; Katherine Brown, ""The Black Athlete" SI Cover July 1, 1968," *Magazines*, https://omeka.middlebury.edu/magazines/items/show/16, 17; Susan Wood/Archive Photos/Getty Images, 18; RLFE Pix/Alamy, 19; Marty Lederhandler/AP Images, 20–21; Mark Brown/Getty Images Entertainment/Getty Images, 23; Evan Agostini/Liaison/Hulton Archive/Getty Images, 25; Focus on Sport/Getty Images, 26–27; Eugene Garcia/AFP/Getty Images, 28; George Gojkovich/Getty Images Sport/Getty Images, 30; Dennis Oulds/Central Press/Hulton Archive/Getty Images, 31; Paul Liebhardt/Corbis Historical/Getty Images, 32; Timothy T Ludwig/Getty Images Sport/Getty Images, 34–35; Christopher Morris/Corbis Sport/Getty Images, 36; Bettmann/Getty Images, 39; Mark Lennihan/AP Images, 41

Editors: Priscilla An and Steph Giedd
Series Designer: Ryan Gale

Library of Congress Control Number: 2022948904

Publisher's Cataloging-in-Publication Data

Names: Radley, Gail, author.
Title: Sports Illustrated: leader in sports media / by Gail Radley
Other title: leader in sports media
Description: Minneapolis, Minnesota: Abdo Publishing Company, 2024 | Series: Big sports brands | Includes online resources and index.
Identifiers: ISBN 9781098290702 (lib. bdg.) | ISBN 9781098276881 (ebook)
Subjects: LCSH: Sports illustrated--Juvenile literature. | Sports--Equipment and supplies--Juvenile literature. | Brand name products--Juvenile literature. | Fan magazines--Juvenile literature.
Classification: DDC 658.827--dc23

TABLE OF CONTENTS

Chapter One
SPORTS ILLUSTRATED SCORES WITH READERS............... 4

Chapter Two
TIME FOR *SPORTS ILLUSTRATED*................ 12

Chapter Three
WHEN A MAGAZINE ISN'T JUST A MAGAZINE 20

Chapter Four
GOOD NEWS AND BAD................ 26

Chapter Five
DOING WHAT THEY DO BEST 34

TIMELINE 42
IMPORTANT PEOPLE 44
GLOSSARY 46
MORE INFORMATION 47
ONLINE RESOURCES 47
INDEX 48
ABOUT THE AUTHOR 48

Chapter One

SPORTS ILLUSTRATED SCORES WITH READERS

Angie focused on her laptop screen as her fingers flew across the keys. She was writing an article about the girls' basketball team for her school's newspaper. She had a deadline to meet, but she needed a break. A copy of her dad's *Sports Illustrated* magazine lay on the coffee table.

She picked up the magazine and leafed through its slick, bright pages filled with athletes. There were football players, a golfer, and some basketball players. But what she admired most were the words on the pages. Angie wanted to be a sports journalist someday like the writers in *Sports Illustrated*.

The play known as "The Longest Yard" from Super Bowl XXXIV was rated by *Sports Illustrated* as one of the 100 greatest moments in sports history.

Tennis icon Serena Williams was first featured on the cover of *Sports Illustrated* in 1999.

She continued to flip through the magazine and saw an interview with basketball star LeBron James. She turned a few more pages to a section called "Faces in the Crowd." Two teenage girls smiled as they kicked a soccer ball across a field. Sisters Gisele and Alyssa Thompson were well-known athletes at just 17 and 18 years old. Maybe Angie could be featured as a Kids Reporter for *Sports Illustrated Kids* by the time she turned 17.

As she continued dreaming of her future, she arrived at the end of the magazine. Angie found an article about tennis player Serena Williams, her favorite athlete. She thought about how cool it would be to interview someone like Williams someday. Angie knew if she worked hard, she could make it happen and write for a magazine like *Sports Illustrated*. But for now, she had to get back to work.

Snap!

Walter Iooss Jr. was just 24 years old in 1967 when *Sports Illustrated* sent him to cover an important football game. It was the just-created pro football championship game that would later become known as Super Bowl I. Iooss knew *Sports Illustrated*, which is sometimes called *SI*, wanted the photos that he snapped fast. There were no computers or cell phones in those days. So, the magazine hired two airplanes for him. Halfway through the game, he took his film to the first plane. The plane flew it from California to the magazine's office in New York. When the game was over, Iooss raced the rest of the film to the

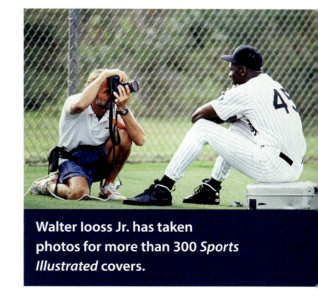

Walter Iooss Jr. has taken photos for more than 300 *Sports Illustrated* covers.

second plane. "The getaway was the most important part of the game," he said. "No film, no job."

His boss knew he could count on Iooss for important jobs. Iooss began taking pictures for *SI* when he was only 17. At 20 he was already taking cover shots.

In 1987 he was assigned to take pictures of basketball star Michael Jordan. Would Jordan wear red or white? Iooss didn't know. He painted half of the court red. He painted the other half blue. Jordan wore red. So Iooss snapped him on the blue side. But first, he rose high above Jordan on a crane. He took photos as Jordan dunked basketballs. The photo that appeared in the magazine was called "The Blue Dunk."

Iooss is known all over the world because his photos stand out. Some photos captured game action. Others were thoughtful portraits. While taking pictures for *SI* over 60 years, he had more than 300 cover photos. He worked with top athletes like Serena Williams, Tiger Woods, and Kobe Bryant. *SI* hires the best, and Iooss set a high bar for them. The magazine's photos are the first thing many people notice about *SI*.

Tell Me a Story

Pictures tell a story. But there's more to an event than a picture can tell. *Sports Illustrated* wants the best writers to match its

Former president Barack Obama, *right*, awarded Frank Deford the National Humanities Medal in 2013.

award-winning photos. Frank Deford started writing for the magazine in 1962. He stayed for 46 years. *SI* calls his stories "the stuff of legends." An *SI* article called Deford "the best sportswriter in America." Other writers agreed. They named him National Sportswriter of the Year six times. Deford didn't just report on sports news. He made readers feel as if they knew the people who made the news. He created pictures with his words so readers could see an athlete's dimples or smashed nose. He told readers what sort of house an athlete lived in

9

and with whom. He let readers hear the athletes speak. Many top writers followed his lead. They helped make *SI* sports fans' first choice.

Melissa Segura got her start writing for *SI* in 2001. She was still in college. She soon showed the magazine she was ready to join the team. Segura helped discover a secret about the Little League World Series. One team's star player, Danny Almonte, should not have been playing. Little Leaguers can't be more than 12 years old, and Almonte was 14. Soon after her reporting, Segura was offered a full-time job. She became one of a growing number of women on staff.

Covering All the Bases

Sports Illustrated reports that it has an audience of nearly 12 million people. They count on the magazine to cover important sports events. They look forward to its special stories and regular pieces. For example, "Faces in the Crowd" and "Point After" are part of every issue. The first is about amateur athletes. "Point After" is a short article with a big picture on the last page. Along with those who read *SI*, many more enjoy *SI*'s other products, including its website. "This brand is on fire right now," said Dan Dienst, the vice chairman of Authentic Brands Group (ABG), the company that owns *Sports Illustrated*.

After Danny Almonte's birth certificate was revealed, his team was disqualified from playing in the Little League World Series.

Chapter Two

TIME FOR SPORTS ILLUSTRATED

Henry Luce was born in China and spent his childhood there. Nevertheless, he had a strong sense of being American. His father would tell him that Americans were not selfish; they always helped others. As a child, Luce loved reading the many books in their home. He was inspired by the American newspapers and magazines that came in the mail, and he wrote his own newspaper for the family. His father told Luce that he had "Lucepower." He said to use it for good.

In 1923, just three years after finishing college in the United States, Luce and a classmate started a

Henry Luce hugely impacted the publishing world with his magazines.

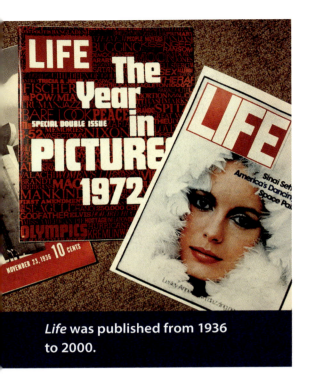

Life was published from 1936 to 2000.

news magazine called *Time*. After that, Luce started *Fortune*, a business magazine, in 1930. *Fortune* and *Time* are still being sold. Luce's second wife, Clare Boothe Luce, encouraged Luce to buy the dying humor magazine *Life* and turn it into a weekly magazine focused on pictures. In 1936 he finally did. The picture focus was a hit. *Life* lasted for 64 years.

Sports Illustrated Is Born

Sports Illustrated was not founded until 1954. Luce was restless to start another magazine. He had been thinking about it for a decade or so. He complained to his partners, "We have $10 million sitting idle." What topics hadn't he tried? Fashion? Children? Or maybe sports. Sports had been talked about before but was dropped. Most people didn't think highly of sports then. Good writers didn't write about sports. Nobody but Luce seemed to like the idea. It "just won't work," a writer said when he quit the project. Athletes, he added, were "dull" and "a little nasty."

Luce kept working on the magazine anyway. He didn't know much about sports. He didn't play or watch them. Still, the time seemed right for a sports magazine. "Man is an animal that works, plays, and prays," he told his staff. Anything that was part of people's lives was important. Sports should be respected. He would lift them up with a well-done magazine.

SI's first issue went on sale on August 16, 1954. It drew interest with a cover shot of Milwaukee Braves baseball player Eddie Mathews taking an at-bat. But there was no story inside to go with the photo. The magazine was slow to make money. A major problem was that it covered inaccessible sports. Few people could afford golf, fox hunting, or yachting. The sports most people played or watched were missing. Someone thinking of placing an ad in *SI* called the magazine "too snooty" and went elsewhere. But readers liked how it was written.

Earning Its Keep

Things began to look better for *Sports Illustrated* in 1960. André Laguerre became its head editor. Laguerre loved both good writing and sports. He saw that football was becoming popular. Various other sports were blossoming all over the country too. By then, most American homes had TVs. TV helped the excitement grow. If *SI* was to succeed, Laguerre thought, it needed to cover popular sports. TV showed the games.

SI would tell the stories behind them and help fans get to know the athletes, their coaches, and the teams. Laguerre drew readers to the stories with full-color photos.

In 1964 Laguerre had an idea that would draw readers for decades to come. At the time, there weren't a lot of sports to write about during the winter months. To help fill the pages, the magazine ran travel stories. Readers welcomed stories about warm beaches. Laguerre could pair a story like this with a cover shot of a woman in a swimsuit. The Swimsuit Issue was born. It quickly became the best-selling issue.

Article ideas also came from current events. For years, Black athletes were not allowed to play with or against white athletes in many sports. That began to slowly change in the late 1940s. By the late 1960s, Black athletes such as tennis player Arthur Ashe and college basketball star Lew Alcindor (now Kareem Abdul-Jabbar) had risen to the top of their sports. Everyone was watching these exciting players. Most white

First Year, Bannister First

A college student was the first person to run a mile in under four minutes. Roger Bannister of the United Kingdom trained hard for running just as he trained to be a neurologist. Then, just 46 days later, Australian John Landy broke Bannister's record. In its first issue, *Sports Illustrated* covered an August 1954 race between the two. Bannister won.

Americans thought that racism in sports was over. But Black athletes knew the issues they still faced everywhere. *SI* ran a five-part series in July 1968 called "The Black Athlete: A Shameful Story." It told the story of lower pay, fewer benefits, and poor treatment for Black athletes. *SI* was the first national magazine to show readers that racism still affected sports. It was a groundbreaking work highlighting racial injustice and inequality in sports. *SI* ran similar series about the effects of drugs, technology, and women's rights in sports.

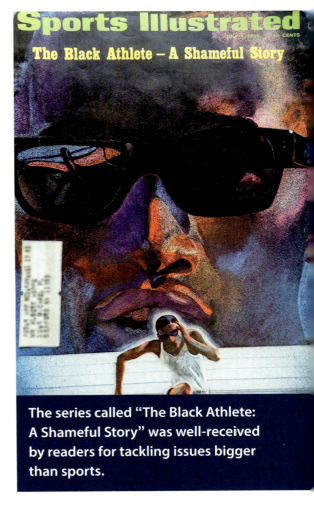

The series called "The Black Athlete: A Shameful Story" was well-received by readers for tackling issues bigger than sports.

Laguerre guided *SI* through some difficult times until 1974. He also "rescued it from financial ruin," wrote Frank Deford. Many people believed *SI* had the best writing and was the best-run magazine under Luce's company, Time Inc. *SI* more than doubled its number of readers with Laguerre's help. It was a golden time for *SI*. But it didn't last forever.

People in Manhattan, New York, thumb through the first issue of *Sports Illustrated*.

Who Has *Sports Illustrated* Now?

After Laguerre, *SI* had other editors. But the writers' joy in their work seemed to be slipping. It was hard for them to accept new bosses. Even so, *SI* won the National Magazine Award for general excellence in 1989 and 1990.

In 1990 the company was sold, and Time Inc. joined Warner Communications, becoming Time Warner, the world's biggest media and entertainment company. The new owners lowered the magazine's costs by cutting staff, making the magazine smaller, and using cheaper paper. They also created videos, calendars, and books inspired by the Swimsuit Issue. However, critics felt that *SI* should stick to magazines, arguing that the spin-offs distracted readers.

In 2014 Time Inc. left Time Warner. It seemed like an opportunity for Time Inc. to pay more attention to its magazines. But four years later, Time Inc. was sold again. *SI* was losing readers and dropped to two issues a month. Then ABG became *SI*'s new owner in 2019. ABG then struck a deal with TheMaven (now Arena Group). *SI* went from publishing weekly magazines to monthly. With the changes, some thought *SI* was dying. But ABG vice chairman Dan Dienst stated, "It's still the most trusted, best brand in sports."

SI has grown with the times, allowing fans to follow sports on their computers and smartphones. Aside from the magazine, *SI*'s other businesses are also successful, at least in part, because of *Sports Illustrated*'s good name.

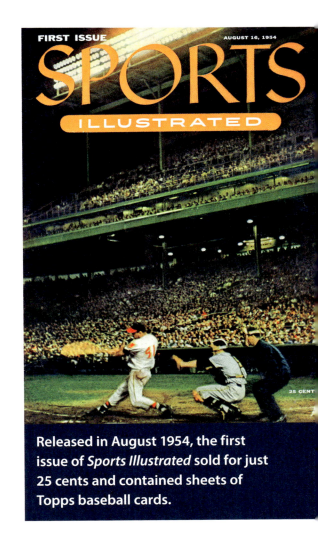

Released in August 1954, the first issue of *Sports Illustrated* sold for just 25 cents and contained sheets of Topps baseball cards.

Chapter Three

WHEN A MAGAZINE ISN'T JUST A MAGAZINE

One way to keep *Sports Illustrated* alive in people's minds has been to grow the brand beyond its paper covers. *Sports Illustrated* is the leader in sports magazines. Over the years, several smaller sports magazines teamed up with *SI*, including *The Hockey News* and *Morning Read*, a golf magazine. As a group, they are called Sports Illustrated Media Group. As of 2022, their combined earnings kept them among the top sports media groups in the country.

Sports Illustrated for Kids started in 1988, a natural spin-off from *SI*. Its name was later shortened to

Sports Illustrated Kids magazine also has a website, sikids.com, which includes articles written by Kid Reporters.

PREMIER ISSUE · JANUARY 1989 $1.75

Sports Illustrated FOR KIDS

JUMP!

NBA SUPERSTAR
MICHAEL JORDAN
WITH FRIENDS
BRAD PIELET AND
NANCY DELLER

Sports Illustrated Kids, but more often it's called *SI Kids*. *SI Kids* is for eight- to 13-year-olds. The new magazine faced 47 other magazines trying to grab kids' attention. The company hoped its readers would graduate to reading *SI*. It also hoped *SI Kids* would be a moneymaker. The company initially printed 500,000 copies, half of which were given away to school libraries.

SI Kids was a success. In seven years, it became a leader in children's magazines, selling about a million copies. The spin-off magazine was so successful that an *SI Kids* TV show was released in 1997. The show featured popular athletes as guests. It also had a space for kids to talk about the pressures they faced in their lives.

Another way of capturing young fans is through social media. The application Snapchat, which came out in 2011, was a natural choice because of its popularity with young people. *SI* launched *America's Best Sports Videos* on Snapchat in late 2021. Users can share their own clips of sports events. Other spin-offs for kids include books, a website, videos, and video games.

The parent magazine, *Sports Illustrated*, has a similar set

Card Play

SI Kids includes a page of trading cards. These aim to show male and female athletes in all sorts of sports. There are surfers and runners, amateurs and pros. Collectors have sold rare early cards for hundreds of thousands of dollars.

Sports Illustrated worked with stores like JCPenney to sell *SI*'s clothing line. Models show off the clothes at the JCPenney Fashion Show during the 2021 Sports Illustrated Awards.

of spin-offs. Although the magazine now comes out only once a month, fans can get the latest news from the podcast *Sports Illustrated Weekly*. While listening to the podcast, they can also learn about well-known athletes past and present.

SI teamed up with a production company to form Sports Illustrated Studios in 2020. It makes TV shows, films, and long podcasts.

High Jump into the Unexpected

Some offshoots, such as clothing, don't have such clear links to *Sports Illustrated*. In its earliest days, the magazine had stories on sports fashion. Its first step into selling fashion was a by-product of the Swimsuit Issue. Some female readers wanted to buy the suits they saw. *SI* partnered with a clothing company to sell swimsuits in 2017.

SI also began partnering with clothing companies to promote its brand, selling clothing such as leggings made for all sizes and body types. In 2021 *SI* teamed up with JCPenney to sell clothing for men, women, and children starting in 2022. Hard Rock, Forever 21, and other companies also sell *SI* clothing.

The new Sports Illustrated Hotels and Resorts business is a jump even further from *SI*. The first vacation spot was planned for the Dominican Republic in 2023. *SI* chose Storyland Studios to plan the resort. Storyland planned to create sports stories in which guests could take part. The attraction was intended to cater to both adults and children. Another resort, in Orlando, Florida, was planned to open in 2024. *SI* officials said they hoped to build many resorts.

Tyra Banks, a model, poses at an event to promote the 33rd *SI Swimsuit Issue* in 1996. She appeared on the cover of this issue with another model, Valeria Mazza.

Chapter Four

GOOD NEWS AND BAD

National Basketball Association (NBA) legend Michael Jordan retired from the sport three separate times. "Now I guess it hits me that I'm not going to be in a uniform anymore," he said when he finally left the game for good in 2003. "It's something I've come to grips with, and it's time." It's hard to walk away from success. Jordan had plenty of it. He set a record by being named NBA Finals Most Valuable Player six times. NBA.com called him "the greatest basketball player of all time."

Michael Jordan first graced the cover of *Sports Illustrated* when he was in college at the University of North Carolina. Jordan has more *SI* covers than any other athlete, with 50.

Success goes a long way in making an athlete like Jordan popular. But so does publicity. Without it, only those who saw him play live would know what he could do. Publicity helps fans become drawn to their favorite players and teams. That helps sell tickets to games and keeps sports alive. Publicity also helps athletes get deals endorsing products. It can help them build new careers when they retire too. *Sports Illustrated* is a great source of sports publicity.

In 2013 Jordan was on the *SI* cover for the 50th time. No athlete has appeared there so many times. With few exceptions, only the best get on *SI*'s covers. A cover shot is an honor and a career booster for most athletes.

Curveball

Success and publicity go together. Athletes usually want their good moves talked about. But no one likes bad publicity. On a break from basketball in 1994, Jordan tried baseball. A *Sports Illustrated* article slammed his poor playing.

Michael Jordan tried baseball with the Chicago White Sox during his first retirement from basketball.

Jordan stopped talking with anyone from *SI*. Years later, the writer said he was too hard on the star. Jordan hadn't put years into playing baseball as he had basketball. And even skilled athletes make mistakes. Writers and photographers cover both the good and the bad.

Even good publicity puts pressure on athletes. When athletes do especially well, fans expect them to keep it up or do even better. The pressure can play on the athletes' minds. For example, when NBA superstar LeBron James was in high school, *SI* put him on the cover with the headline "The Chosen One." There have been questions since then about whether it was fair to put that pressure on James at such a young age.

Sports Illustrated Cover Jinx?

For all the good that being on *Sports Illustrated*'s cover seems to offer, some people think it is a jinx. They point to a curious trend of negative things happening to people who make the cover. Often, the person performs badly, or their team loses a game. For example, tennis star John McEnroe surprised everyone by losing the 1984 ATP championship after a cover shot. In the same year, "Man of Steel" linebacker Jack Lambert had a toe injury that eventually ended his career. Sometimes, it's more serious. In 1962 race car driver Ricardo Rodríguez was killed in a crash. And the 50 covers featuring Jordan didn't seem to hurt his game, but he was sued for divorce after one of them.

Still, it isn't just the *Sports Illustrated* cover that seems to jinx athletes. The same has been said about baseball's Cy Young Award and the cover of a video game, *Madden NFL*. Professor Gary Smith said athletes need luck as well as skill to earn a place on the cover. But after they've done their best, "there is . . . nowhere to go but down." In other words, a run of luck can't last forever. It's still rare for an athlete to turn down an *SI* cover shot.

Celebrate!

An award can be powerful recognition for the people who earn it. *Sports Illustrated* has given many of them, the first in 1954. It named Roger Bannister, the British runner who broke the four-minute mile, Sportsman of the Year.

Linebacker Jack Lambert was the National Football League (NFL) Defensive Player of the Year in 1976.

Billie Jean King won 39 major tennis titles in her career.

It wasn't until 1972 that a Sports*woman* of the Year was named. Tennis champ Billie Jean King had to share the honor with basketball coach John Wooden, who was named Sportsman of the Year. However, in 1976, no sportsman shared the spotlight with sportswoman Chris Evert, another tennis player. In 2015 Serena Williams became Sports*person* of the Year. From that point on, the honor no longer suggested that the athlete was top among men or among women. The sportsperson is honored among *all* athletes. As *SI* summed it up in a 2022 press release, the title "is an honor for athletes, coaches, and teams who best represent the spirit and ideals of sportsmanship, character, and performance, given annually since the inception of *Sports Illustrated*."

Some athletes are recognized for success over longer periods. In 1999 *SI* gave boxer Muhammad Ali the Sportsman of the Century Legacy Award. Ali had been named heavyweight champion three times. He inspired thousands of young people in the ring and outside it as a civil rights activist.

SI wanted to honor other athletes who, like Ali, work to make the world better. The first Sportsman Legacy Award was given in 2008 to Eunice Shriver for her work starting the Special Olympics. This sports program allows people with intellectual disabilities to compete. In 2015 *SI* honored the boxing champ again by renaming the award the *Sports Illustrated* Muhammad Ali Legacy Award.

Muhammad Ali shows off his *SI* cover feature before his fight with Jimmy Ellis in July 1971.

Golfer Jack Nicklaus was the first to win the renamed award. Allyson Felix, an Olympic track star, was the 2022 winner.

Calling All Female Athletes

Sports Illustrated offered all female athletes the chance to win a spot on the cover of the June 2022 issue. Once, women had few opportunities to play sports. That changed in the United States with the passing of a law called Title IX. The law states that girls should have the same opportunities at school as boys. That includes sports. As an *SI* editor said, Title IX helped women and girls "grow as leaders on and off the field." To celebrate Title IX's 50th birthday, *SI* invited women to send photos and stories of how the law had helped them. The cover was a collage of female athletes. It was also a welcome bit of publicity to bring women's sports into the spotlight.

Two Firsts

Sports Illustrated ran its first cover with a Black woman in 1957. It featured tennis champ Althea Gibson. She often competed where Black people once weren't allowed. She was also the first Black athlete to win a Grand Slam event when she won the 1957 French Championships (now the French Open).

Chapter Five

DOING WHAT THEY DO BEST

As part of keeping up with the computer age, *Sports Illustrated* got into fantasy sports. According to a study published in 2014, more than 41 million people from the United States and Canada play fantasy sports. "We cover fantasy sports, we write about it," said Jim DeLorenzo, the vice president and general manager of SI Digital, "but the thing that's been a hole in our digital product suite has been an actual fantasy game."

SI's leap into fantasy began with fantasy football. The game lets players put together the team of their dreams by choosing real NFL athletes. Players win

> On January 12, 2023, Buffalo Bills quarterback Josh Allen was ranked number one in *Sports Illustrated*'s fantasy football player rankings.

The US women's soccer team was featured on the cover of *Sports Illustrated* after its World Cup win in 2015.

based on how many points their athletes earn in real games each week. Golf, baseball, and other sports also have fantasy games. Many fantasy players rely on the sort of daily news *SI* was already offering on its website.

For a time, there was a downside to *SI*'s involvement with fantasy games. At one time *SI* worked with the NFL, which created a fantasy game tailored toward children aged six to 12. It offered prizes to winners. The games were even pushed through elementary school lessons. However, the fantasy games, wrote one critic, "may encourage children to spend excessive amounts of time trying to win these prizes, thus planting the seeds of addiction." Finally, the protests from concerned groups led the NFL and *SI* to stop targeting children.

The Swimsuit Debate

The ever-popular Swimsuit Issue has also stirred protests. *Sports Illustrated* once carried beach travel articles. So those first Swimsuit Issues made some sense. But when the travel pieces stopped, the Swimsuit Issue stayed. Many people wondered why. The women shown were not athletes. They were simply pretty women wearing swimsuits. Psychology professor Elizabeth Daniels found that the type of photos *SI* uses in its magazines makes women and girls feel bad about their own bodies.

Professor Cynthia M. Frisby studied four years' worth of covers from *SI* and another sports magazine. She wanted to see how often female athletes were shown. She also wondered *how* they were shown. Passing Title IX led to many more female athletes, she noted. But for every 10 covers, only one pictured a woman. Men and women were also not shown the

Ballers *and* Beauties

In May 2022, the Swimsuit Issue featured only Women's National Basketball Association (WNBA) players on the cover to celebrate the WNBA's 25th anniversary. Former Seattle Storm guard Sue Bird said, "We represent a variety of things: of course women, women of color, members of the LGBTQIA2+ community and much more. . . . The [Swimsuit] issue for so many years has been iconic and has represented a lot for women. Now you are seeing an evolution in what that can mean and what that can look like."

same way. Men were usually seen in action, wearing their uniforms. They appeared strong and skillful. The female shots, though, often gave no clue they were athletes. Most shots were posed. The athletes were rarely shown in uniform. In fact, sometimes female athletes were shown wearing swimsuits. The photos did not depict the strong, skilled athletes that *SI* covers are otherwise known for promoting.

With the January 2022 issue, *SI* announced it would honor the Swimsuit Issue's 58th anniversary by using it to empower women. *SI* promised to sell ads only to companies with programs that help women advance. It would also donate part of the issue's earnings to a group working on those goals. What *SI* didn't promise was to do away with the swimsuit models, as the issue brings in a lot of revenue. Professor Daniels felt *SI* could have done better. "The best thing *Sports Illustrated* could do for women would

Budd Schulberg was a boxing editor, novelist, and screenwriter credited with exposing the lies behind some boxing matches.

be to cover women's sports and to cover women athletes, as athletes," she said.

Digging Out the Bad Guys

Sports Illustrated's actions have sometimes troubled people. But *SI* has also done much to help sports. As early as 1954, *SI* reporters were digging deep to uncover unfair and illegal actions. Budd Schulberg was *SI*'s first boxing editor. That first year, he and a team looked into how boxing matches were arranged. They found that some fights were rigged, or fixed. In other words, boxers were paid to lose their matches. Gamblers were sure of winning bets since the winner was picked in advance. Schulberg's story showed that fans weren't always seeing real matches. Once the story was out, the number of fixed fights was greatly reduced.

In 1969 *SI* writer Bil Gilbert wrote a three-part series on drug use in sports. At that time, only those inside sports knew that athletes were taking dangerous drugs to play better, sometimes with their coaches' urging. Gilbert's articles drew much interest. Other publications tackled the topic with their own articles. *SI*'s articles also inspired the federal government to look at the problem, along with various sports organizations.

SI followed up with other articles, including "The Nightmare of Steroids" in 1988. The piece told the story of football lineman Tommy Chaikin. These articles helped bring about changes in sports to protect the athletes and make the contests fair, but the drug problem is still far from over.

Into the Future

As *Sports Illustrated* makes plans for its future, its leaders can't help but consider its past. *SI* has been on the sports scene since 1954. It has covered some of the greatest moments in

Authentic Brand Group purchased *Sports Illustrated* in 2019 for $110 million.

sports history. "To this day," wrote the editors in 2021, "we take our audience deeper inside the game and closer to the biggest names in sports than anyone else."

SI is a magazine first. It wants to hold on to the deep stories and eye-catching photos that made fans love it. *SI* has grown and changed in ways Henry Luce could never have imagined. It is now a brand with a batch of spin-off products for all sorts of interests. Once it aimed to please readers who were wealthy white men. Now *Sports Illustrated* is stretching to reach a much wider audience while continuing its tradition of bringing fans deeper into the sports they love.

41

TIMELINE

1954
The first issue of *Sports Illustrated* goes on sale on August 16.

1960
André Laguerre becomes managing editor, gradually turning *SI* into a profitable magazine.

1968
In July *SI* runs a five-part series exposing injustices against Black athletes.

1974
Laguerre leaves *SI* after more than doubling its number of readers during his time with the magazine.

1989 and 1990
SI wins the National Magazine Award for general excellence two years in a row.

1990
SI's owner, Time Inc., merges with Warner Communications to become Time Warner.

2014
Time Inc. separates from Time Warner.

2018
SI reduces issues to twice a month.

2019
Authentic Brands Group purchases *SI*. Arena Group then acquires the magazine, and issues are reduced to one per month the following year.

2022
In June *SI* honors the 50th birthday of Title IX by releasing a cover featuring female athletes of all ages and abilities.

IMPORTANT PEOPLE

Muhammad Ali

In 1999 SI named boxing champion Muhammad Ali Athlete of the Century, not only because of being the heavyweight champion three times but because he was active in the civil rights struggle and helped others recognize Black people as equals. *SI* also renamed its Sportsman Legacy Award after Ali in 2015.

Frank Deford

Frank Deford was a storyteller who gave readers in-depth descriptions of athletes on and off their playing surfaces. A model for other sportswriters for years to come, he wrote for *SI* from 1962 to 1989 and from 1998 until his death in 2017.

Walter Iooss Jr.

Photographer Walter Iooss Jr. began taking pictures for *SI* when he was only 17 years old. Iooss photographed the first Super Bowl. During his six decades with the magazine, he took more than 300 cover photos and worked with many top athletes.

Michael Jordan

Michael Jordan has been called "the greatest basketball player of all time" by the NBA. *SI* showed him on its cover 50 times, more than any other athlete.

André Laguerre

André Laguerre was hired by Henry Luce to turn *SI* into a moneymaking magazine. He became managing editor in 1960, staying until 1974. He not only helped double readership but also created a more exciting, modern work.

Henry Luce

Henry Luce, the cofounder of *Time* magazine, went on to start *Sports Illustrated* and several other magazines. Although Luce knew little about sports, he knew they were important to people and believed that skilled writers should write about them.

Melissa Segura

Melissa Segura began at *SI* as a college intern in 2001 and became a full-time *SI* writer in 2002. She later went on to write for Buzzfeed.

Serena Williams

Serena Williams was named *SI*'s first Sportsperson of the Year in 2015. The tennis star first appeared on the cover of *SI* in 1999.

GLOSSARY

annually
Occurring every year.

decade
A span of 10 years.

financial
Refers to finances or money.

issue
A single edition of a series. Magazine issues are often published monthly.

legacy
Something of importance that came from someone in the past.

legend
A player who is generally regarded as one of the best to ever play.

media
Various forms of passing along information, such as magazines, film, etc.

podcast
An audio program given in digital form so it can be downloaded over the internet.

publish
To make available to the public—for example, when a writer's words are turned into a book others can read.

racism
Discriminating against other people based only on their race.

yachting
Racing, sailing, or traveling in a large boat.

MORE INFORMATION

BOOKS

Dyer, Kristian R. *ESPN: Top Sports Channel*. Minneapolis, MN: Abdo Publishing, 2024.

Hewson, Anthony K. *Serena Williams*. Minneapolis, MN: Abdo Publishing, 2024.

Rowell, Rebecca. *Gatorade: Sports Drink Innovator*. Minneapolis, MN: Abdo Publishing, 2024.

ONLINE RESOURCES

To learn more about *Sports Illustrated*, please visit **abdobooklinks.com** or scan this QR code. These links are routinely monitored and updated to provide the most current information available.

INDEX

Alcindor, Lew, 16
  Abdul-Jabbar, Kareem, 16
Ali, Muhammad, 32–33
Almonte, Danny, 10
Ashe, Arthur, 16

Bannister, Roger, 16, 30–31
Bird, Sue, 38
Boothe Luce, Clare, 14
Bryant, Kobe, 8

Chaikin, Tommy, 40

Daniels, Elizabeth, 37–38
Deford, Frank, 8–9, 17
Dienst, Dan, 10, 19

Evert, Chris, 31

Felix, Allyson, 33
Frisby, Cynthia M., 37

Gibson, Althea, 33
Gilbert, Bil, 40

Iooss, Walter, Jr., 7–8

James, LeBron, 6, 29
Jordan, Michael, 7, 8, 26, 28–30

King, Billie Jean, 31

Laguerre, André, 15–18
Lambert, Jack, 29
Luce, Henry, 12–15, 17, 41

Mathews, Eddie, 15
McEnroe, John, 29

National Basketball Association (NBA), 26, 29
National Football League (NFL), 30, 34, 36–37
Nicklaus, Jack, 33

Rodríguez, Ricardo, 29

Schulberg, Budd, 39–40
Segura, Melissa, 10
Shriver, Eunice, 32
Smith, Gary, 30
Swimsuit Issue, 16, 18, 24, 25, 37–38

Title IX, 33, 37

Williams, Serena, 7–8, 31
Wooden, John, 31
Woods, Tiger, 8

ABOUT THE AUTHOR

Gail Radley is the author of more than 40 books for young people. She lives in DeLand, Florida, and loves swimming and walking in the woods.